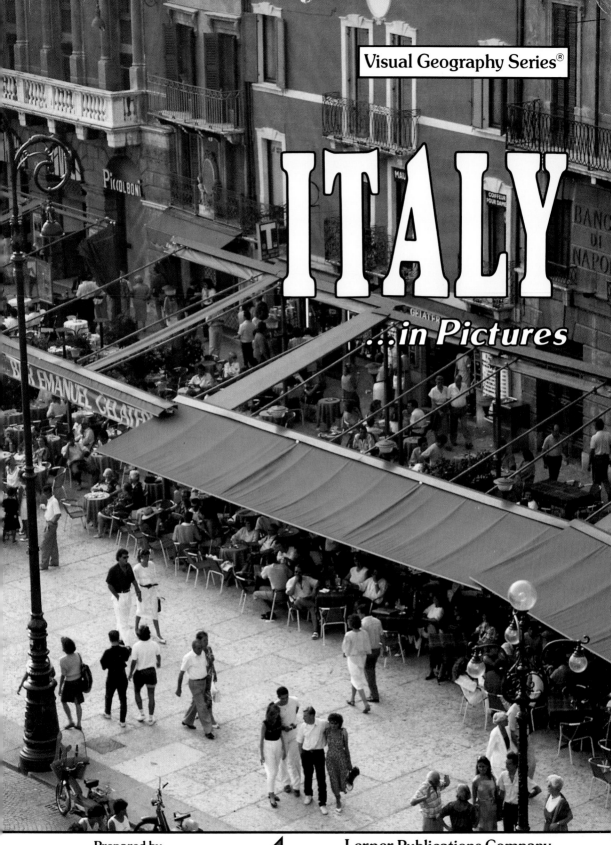

Visual Geography Series®

ITALY

...in Pictures

Prepared by
Geography Department

Lerner Publications Company
Minneapolis

VISUAL GEOGRAPHY SERIES®

Publisher
Harry Jonas Lerner
Senior Editor
Mary M. Rodgers
Editors
Joan Freese
Colleen Sexton
Photo Researcher
Beth Johnson
Consultants/Contributors
Tom Streissguth
John G. Rice
Sandra K. Davis
Designer
Jim Simondet
Cartographer
Carol F. Barrett
Indexer
Sylvia Timian
Production Manager
Gary J. Hansen

A cheering crowd watches an Italian bobsledder careen around a curve.

Independent Picture Service

This book is an all-new edition of the Visual Geography Series. Previous editions were published by Sterling Publishing Company, New York City. The text, set in 10/12 Century Textbook, is fully revised and updated, and new photographs, maps, charts, and captions have been added.

LIBRARY OF CONGRESS CATALOGING-IN-PUBLICATION DATA

Italy in pictures / prepared by Geography Department, Lerner Publications Company.
  p. cm.—(Visual Geography Series)
  Summary: Examines the geography, history, society, economy, and government of Italy.
  Includes index.
  ISBN 0–8225–1884–8 (lib. bdg.)
  1. Italy—Juvenile literature. [1. Italy.] I. Lerner Publications Company. Geography dept. II. Series: Visual geography series (Minneapolis, Minn.)
DT417.I8885 1997
949.4—dc20   95–45609

International Standard Book Number: 0–8225–1884–8
Library of Congress Catalog Card Number: 95–45609

Independent Picture Service

A traditional folk artist paints the side of a cart.

Acknowledgments

Title page photo © Chuck Place

Elevation contours adapted from *The Times Atlas of the World,* seventh comprehensive edition (New York: Times Books, 1985).

1 2 3 4 5 6 – JR – 02 01 00 99 98 97

Tiers of vineyards hug the mountain slopes of northeastern Italy, a region noted for its fine wines.

Contents

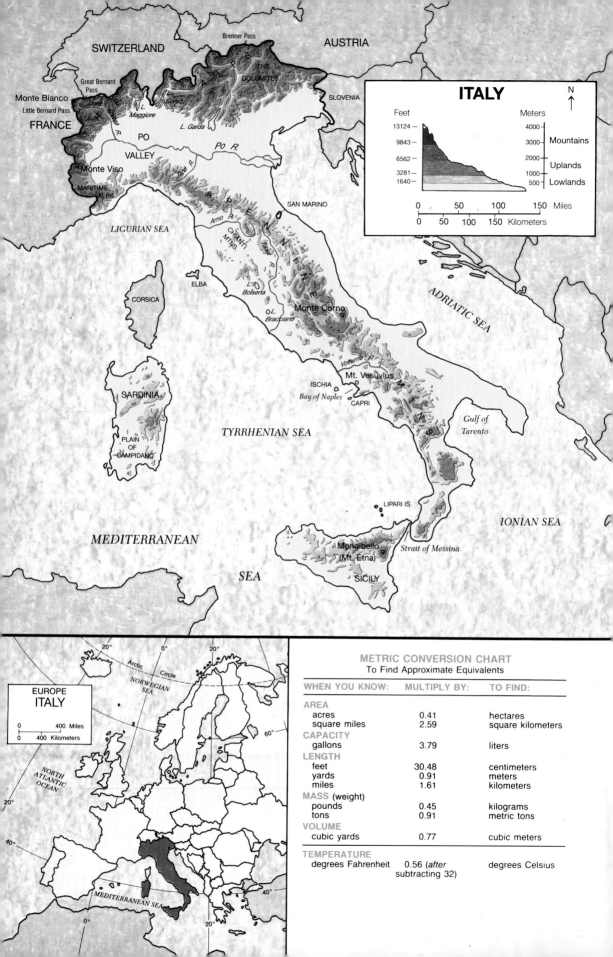

SWITZERLAND

Brenner Pass

AUSTRIA

THE DOLOMITES

ALPS

Monte Bianco

Great Bernard Pass

SLOVENIA

Little Bernard Pass

FRANCE

L. Maggiore

Sesia R.

L. Garda

Ticino R.

PO VALLEY

PO R.

Monte Viso

Taro R.

MARITIME ALPS

APENNINES

SAN MARINO

LIGURIAN SEA

Arno R.

CHIANTI MTNS.

Tiber R.

ELBA

L. Bolsena

CORSICA

L. Bracciano

Monte Corno

ADRIATIC SEA

Volturno R.

SARDINIA

ISCHIA

Mt. Vesuvius

Bay of Naples

CAPRI

Gulf of Tarento

PLAIN OF CAMPIDANO

TYRRHENIAN SEA

MEDITERRANEAN

LIPARI IS.

SEA

IONIAN SEA

Mongibello (Mt. Etna)

Strait of Messina

SICILY

ITALY

N ↑

Feet		Meters	
13124 —		4000 —	
9843 —		3000 —	Mountains
6562 —		2000 —	
3281 —		1000 —	Uplands
1640 —		500 —	Lowlands

0   50   100   150   Miles
0   50   100   150   Kilometers

EUROPE
ITALY

0   400 Miles
0   400 Kilometers

Arctic Circle

NORWEGIAN SEA

NORTH ATLANTIC OCEAN

MEDITERRANEAN SEA

20° 0° 20° 60° 40° 0°

METRIC CONVERSION CHART
To Find Approximate Equivalents

WHEN YOU KNOW:	MULTIPLY BY:	TO FIND:
AREA		
acres	0.41	hectares
square miles	2.59	square kilometers
CAPACITY		
gallons	3.79	liters
LENGTH		
feet	30.48	centimeters
yards	0.91	meters
miles	1.61	kilometers
MASS (weight)		
pounds	0.45	kilograms
tons	0.91	metric tons
VOLUME		
cubic yards	0.77	cubic meters
TEMPERATURE		
degrees Fahrenheit	0.56 (*after* subtracting 32)	degrees Celsius

Photo by M. Bryan Ginsberg

Nestled among trees and rolling farmland, this summer home is a short drive from the bustling city of Venice on Italy's northeastern coast.

Introduction

A European nation with a long history and a rich cultural heritage, Italy is also a surprising economic success story. A few years after the end of World War II (1939–1945), the Italian Republic—as the country is officially known—had transformed itself from a poor and largely agricultural nation into a modern industrial power. Italian companies now produce a wide range of manufactured goods and export their products to Europe, Asia, and North and South America.

But many regions of Italy, especially in the south, remain poor and underdeveloped. As a result, a wide gap between the rich and the poor exists and is worsened by the problems of unemployment and inflation (rising prices).

Italy's leaders have not been successful at correcting these problems. Instead shaky coalition governments that spend only short periods in office have eroded national unity. In addition, many Italians feel more loyalty to their families and neighborhoods than they do to the national government. This lack of interest in traditional political parties has also hampered reforms.

Many of Italy's current troubles are products of its long history. Italy has been a unified nation only since 1861. The center of the powerful Roman Empire 2,000 years ago, the Italian Peninsula broke up

5

into hundreds of small states and private domains after the fall of Rome in the fifth century A.D. In the 1200s, several Italian cities developed new forms of government run by wealthy merchant families. Although they were among the richest communities in Europe, these city-states constantly fought among themselves. Eventually, the peninsula fell under foreign domination, first by Spain and later by Austria and France.

Foreign rule continued until Italy became a state in 1861. The new nation, like much of the rest of Europe, fought in World War I (1914–1918) and in World War II. Invaded during the second global conflict, Italy was left with bombed-out cities and ruined farmland.

Postwar financial aid from the United States led to an explosion in Italy's industrial economy, and the nation experienced two decades of fast growth and increasing prosperity. Yet economic development did not lessen the historic lack of unity among Italy's many historical regions, a situation that had worsened by the early 1990s.

New political parties are supporting increased independence for certain areas of the country, especially in the more prosperous north. By the mid-1990s, this disunity and the lack of trust in Italian leaders and institutions were posing a serious threat to Italy's continuing stability and prosperity. If Italy can overcome these problems, the country faces a bright, productive future.

Dating to about 150 B.C., the ruins of the Roman Forum stand in Rome, the capital of Italy. The Forum's marketplace—an open air structure bordered by arches and columns—was the main public gathering area in ancient Rome. The Forum also included the Roman Senate, courts of law, and other important public buildings, which surrounded this main square.

The towering limestone cliffs of the Dolomites dwarf a small village. The Dolomites are part of the Alps, a mountain range that stretches across much of western Europe, including northern Italy.

1) The Land

The Italian Republic is situated in southern Europe on a long, narrow, boot-shaped peninsula that juts into the Mediterranean Sea. The Alps, Europe's largest mountain range, form the northern boundary of the country. Along this archlike border lie France in the west, Switzerland and Austria in the north, and Slovenia in the east. Two independent states—the republic of San Marino and Vatican City—lie within Italy's borders.

Four seas—each part of the greater Mediterranean—surround the Italian Peninsula. The Adriatic Sea lies to east, while the Ionian Sea divides Italy from Greece in the southeast. The Tyrrhenian Sea lies off Italy's southwestern coast, and waves from the Ligurian Sea lap against the country's northwestern coast.

Italy covers a total of 116,314 square miles. Large and small islands, including Sicily and Sardinia, combine with the mainland to form the total landmass. In area the country is slightly smaller than the state of New Mexico. The greatest length of Italy from northwest to southeast is 708 miles. The country measures 320 miles at its widest point in the north.

Topography

Although three-quarters of Italy's terrain is mountainous, a wide variety of geographical features exists within the country. In addition, Italy is divided into 20 administrative regions. The chief regions of the north are Piedmont, Lombardy, and Venetia; of central Italy are Tuscany, Umbria, and Latium; and of the south are Campania, Basilicata, and Calabria.

These areas follow traditional or historical boundaries but sometimes match specific geographical features. As a result, the description of Italy's landscape often involves the use of regional as well as topographical names.

THE MAINLAND

The Alps dominate northern Italy's terrain as they sweep across central Europe. Many smaller ranges exist within the Alps, including the Maritime Alps, which divide Italy from France in the northwest. Monte Bianco (Mont Blanc in French) straddles

Boaters guide their narrow craft along the Po River, which waters the fertile fields of the Po Valley. This broad plain is Italy's most productive agricultural region.

the French-Italian border, reaching an elevation of 15,771 feet—the highest point in the Alps.

Eastward, between Italy, Switzerland, and Austria, lies a series of Alpine ranges. The Dolomites, for example, near the Austrian border, are notable for their steep, treeless cliffs that dramatically loom over mountain valleys. Northern Italy also features a line of Alpine lakes that were formed tens of thousands of years ago by melting glaciers (moving ice masses). Several glaciers still cover the high valleys of the Dolomites. Travel within the Italian Alps is possible by way of a number of mountain passes, including the Brenner, the Great Bernard, and the Little Bernard.

Alpine foothills gradually run down to the flat and fertile Po Valley, Italy's largest plain, which sits in the north central section of the country. With the exception of its Adriatic coastline, the Po Valley is entirely surrounded by mountains. Watered by the Po River, the valley has been settled and heavily farmed since ancient times and remains the nation's most densely populated region. The west central portion of the plain is Italy's industrial heartland and supports many prosperous

Perched on a steep slope, a small mountain village lies in the Apennines, a rugged range that extends almost the entire length of Italy.

Rolling farmland and thick forests cover Tuscany *(left)*, a region bordering the Apennines on the northwestern peninsula. This rich agricultural area produces much of Italy's grain, livestock, and fruit. Along Italy's southern coast *(below)*, the clear waters of the Mediterranean Sea wash against tall cliffs and sandy shores.

farms. The northeastern valley supports orchards and vineyards that dot the well-watered countryside.

Just south of the Po Valley, the Apennines run in a long north-south band through the central peninsula into southern Italy. Generally lower and less steep than the Alps, the Apennines are thickly forested and host an abundance of wildlife. The mountains reach their highest point at Monte Corno, also known as the Gran Sasso d'Italia.

Palermo—a major seaport and center for shipbuilding—lies on the northwestern coast of Sicily. A large, mountainous island, Sicily has been part of Italy since 1861.

Many smaller ranges parallel the Apennines on both the eastern and western sides of the peninsula. The Chianti Mountains, for example, rise just south of the city of Florence, the capital of Tuscany. In the east, the Apennines are steeper and cling to the coastal plains. On the eastern slope of the Apennines, just south of the coastal town of Rimini, lies the tiny republic of San Marino. Although totally surrounded by Italy, San Marino is a separate nation and not subject to Italian rule.

On the other side of the peninsula, along the Tyrrhenian coast, western plains provide rich farmland, which is second only to the Po Valley in production. In the south, these natural plains are supplemented by *maremme* (drained marshes), which farmers have made into fertile farmland.

A third plain sits on the Adriatic coast in southeastern Italy. Although extremely dry, the soil can be planted, and farmers work plateaus that butt against the cliffs of the Mediterranean coastline. In contrast, the steep hillsides at the southernmost tip of the peninsula support only small, relatively poor farms.

THE ISLANDS

Sicily and Sardinia—the two largest islands in the Mediterranean—belong to Italy. Separated from the mainland by the narrow Strait of Messina, the mountainous island of Sicily includes several rugged plateaus. The island's highest point is Mongibello—also known as Mount Etna—an active volcano near the eastern coast. Sardinia, west of the Italian mainland in the Tyrrhenian Sea, consists of the narrow Plain of Campidano lined on either side by mountains.

Other islands in the Tyrrhenian include the Lipari Islands, which sit north of Sicily; Capri and Ischia, situated near the Bay of Naples; and Elba, off the coast of Tuscany.

11

The Arno River reaches its narrowest point at the Tuscan city of Florence, where the Ponte Vecchio spans the waterway. This famous bridge is lined by the shops of merchants and artisans.

Rivers and Lakes

The Po River—Italy's longest and only navigable river—passes through the nation's largest and most fertile agricultural area. The waterway flows eastward from the Alpine foothills through the lowlands of Lombardy and Venetia.

As the Po approaches the Adriatic Sea, the river branches into a wide delta (a flat piece of land at the mouth of the river). Many tributaries flow into the Po from the Alps on the north and from the Apennines on the south. In the spring, these smaller rivers—such as the Dora Baltea and the Taro—swell with snowmelt and rain from the mountains. Rivers in the Alps and the Apennines have been harnessed for hydroelectric production for nearly a century.

Italy's other major rivers include the Arno—the main waterway of Tuscany—and the Tiber, which drains the countryside of west central Italy around the capital city of Rome. The Volturno is the largest and longest river in Campania.

Several short rivers parallel the eastern slopes of the Apennines, emptying into the Adriatic Sea. These rivers often run dry during the warm summer months.

Thousands of years ago, Alpine glaciers in northern Italy formed a series of long, narrow lakes, including Lake Maggiore, Lake Como, and Lake Garda. In the central portion of the country, Lake Bolsena and Lake Bracciano fill the craters of extinct volcanoes north of Rome. Small mountain lakes dot the Apennines, and other lakes lie along the Adriatic coast. All of these spots attract tourists in the summer.

Climate

Italy's climate varies greatly from region to region. Temperatures and rainfall amounts differ from north to south, from the high mountains to the low valleys, and from the coast to inland areas.

In the Po Valley, damp winters and warm summers are typical. Most rain falls in the spring and autumn. In winter the

Alps and the higher plateaus north of the Po Valley have heavy snowfalls—as much as 30 feet annually. More rain and snow fall in the northeast than in the northwest, where mild, dry winds blow in from the Mediterranean Sea. The city of Milan, on the plain of Lombardy, sees average temperatures of 35° F in January and 74° F in July.

Farther south the climate becomes warmer and drier. At higher elevations, however, temperatures generally are lower and precipitation is heavier than on the coastal plains. In Rome, which lies on the western plain not far from the sea, temperatures average 46° F in January and 78° F in July and August. The Apennines shelter the western coast from cold northerly winds, but the Tyrrhenian coast receives more rainfall than the Adriatic.

Virtually all of coastal Italy has a Mediterranean climate. Rainfall is concentrated in the cool season while the summers are rainless. This type of climate is

Photo © Don Eastman

Skiers find plenty of snow in the Alps *(left)*, while the warm beaches of the southern coast *(below)* draw swimmers and sunbathers.

Photo © Chuck Place

unique and challenging for plants, which require both warmth and water to grow.

Southern Italy and Sicily have dry, warm climates. Summers can be very hot, but winters are mild. Average rainfall varies drastically—from 15 to nearly 40 inches—and is heavier near the coasts than it is in the mountainous interior. A hot and humid wind, called the *sirocco*, blows northward into Italy from the deserts of northern Africa. In the spring, siroccos can even bring dust to southern portions of the Italian Peninsula.

Flora and Fauna

Italy has been settled for thousands of years. As a result, many of its woodlands have been cut down to make room for farms and cities. Yet natural forests still thrive in many of the nation's mountainous regions. The slopes of the Alps support

Photo © Charles Rushing/Visuals Unlimited

Wild goats called ibexes roam Italy's Alpine slopes.

beech, chestnut, and oak trees. Shrubs, mosses, lichens, and many kinds of wildflowers grow above the tree line, where the climate is too extreme to support the growth of trees.

Poplar trees have been planted in the lowlands of the Po Valley, where farming and settlement destroyed nearly all of the original forests. In the Apennines, oak and chestnut forests are common. The dry highlands and coastal areas of the southeastern plain support hardy olive trees, as well as carob trees and Aleppo pines. Scrub vegetation known as maquis grows in deforested regions of southern Italy, Sicily, and Sardinia.

The Alps are home to many of Italy's wild animals, including chamois (a small antelope), black bears, foxes, roe deer, and ibexes. Otters and wildcats live in the Apennines, and a small number of wolves inhabit both central and southern Italy. Moufflon sheep and wild boars thrive in the rugged mountains of Sardinia.

At one time, Italian forests held millions of birds, but extensive hunting over the centuries has driven many species from the area. Wood grouse, ravens, and swallows are still common throughout the country. Although the Mediterranean suffers from pollution, it still shelters sharks, octopi, tuna, swordfish, sponges, and several varieties of coral.

Cities

Italy is a largely urban nation. Throughout history cities have been important political units on the Italian Peninsula. This trend continued in the mid-1990s with almost 97 percent of Italy's 57 million people residing in urban areas. In addition, Rome, Milan, Naples, Florence, and other Italian communities rank among the world's best-known cities.

ROME

Italy's capital and largest city, Rome (population 2.7 million) lies on both sides

A mixture of ancient monuments and grand churches as well as modern buildings and business districts, Rome is known as the Eternal City because of its long history. Legend says that twin brothers Romulus and Remus founded Rome in 753 B.C.

of the Tiber River near the western coastal plain. In the seventh century B.C., Rome began as a collection of small, fortified farming villages that covered several hills near the river's banks. Eventually, Rome expanded, raised powerful armies, and conquered the Italian Peninsula.

During the fifth century A.D., the city came under the control of Roman Catholic popes. Over the following centuries, Rome became the center of the Catholic Church and of a domain known as the Papal States. In 1870, nearly a decade after Italy was unified, Rome was one of the last regions to be incorporated into the new state. (In fact, the Vatican in central Rome has remained the independent domain of the Catholic pope.)

The modern city of Rome has maintained hundreds of monuments, cathe-drals, and public buildings from its past, including the Villa Borghese, a park that was once the estate of a wealthy Roman family. The city hall stands on the Campidoglio, an imposing square designed by Michelangelo, a famous artist of the 1500s. Ancient temples survive in the Roman Forum, once the center of government in ancient Rome.

The political capital of Italy, Rome is also an important hub of business, education, and the arts. The Italian film and television industry, for example, is headquartered on the outskirts of the city. The University of Rome is Italy's largest institution of post-secondary education. Rome hosted the 1960 Summer Olympic Games, for which civic leaders built a massive Sports Palace on the southwestern edge of town. This facility now hosts soccer games.

A popular gathering place in Rome, the Spanish Steps curve from the Fontana della Barcaccia—a fountain at the foot of the steps—to the Church of Santa Trinità dei Monti. From the top, the Spanish Steps offer a sweeping view of the city.

Photo © Chuck Place

SECONDARY CITIES

With a population of 1.6 million, Milan is the second largest city in Italy. Located on the northern plains, Milan is also the nation's business capital and an important European center of banking, service industries, and manufacturing. Founded by Celtic peoples around 400 B.C., Milan prospered from trade with northern Europe during the time of the Roman Empire. Milan grew in importance during the unification of Italy in the 1860s. About a century later, the city's many manufacturing firms drew immigrants from southern Italy.

Modern Milan is the home of Italy's main stock exchange as well as La Scala, a world-famous opera house. The massive Duomo, or cathedral, in the center of town

Photo © Galyn C. Hammond

Milan—a center of business and industry—is Italy's biggest city when combined with the surrounding suburbs. More than four million people live in metropolitan Milan, making it one of the largest cities in Europe.

is adorned with more than 2,000 sculptures and is the third largest church in the world. Milan's Pirelli Tower, a modern glass skyscraper, is the tallest building in Italy.

Naples (population 1.2 million) lies on the north side of the Bay of Naples in southwestern Italy. A manufacturing hub that produces machinery, chemicals, transportation equipment, and textiles, the city also suffers from overcrowding, crime, air pollution, and unemployment.

An age-old political and cultural crossroads, Naples was founded about 600 B.C. by Greek colonists. The city later became a favorite summer resort for wealthy Roman families. Its elaborate cathedrals, ornate palaces, and imposing castles still draw tourists from around the world. Some visitors go to the city's impressive archaeological museum or to the nearby ruins of Pompeii and Herculaneum—ancient Roman towns preserved in ash spewed from the eruptions of Mount Vesuvius in A.D. 79.

Turin (population 1.1 million) lies along the Po River in northwestern Italy. Founded during the Roman Empire, the city grew rapidly during the 1800s when it developed manufacturing industries. Turin served as united Italy's capital from

Crowded residential areas and old castles sit side by side in Naples, an important seaport on Italy's southwestern coast.

1861 to 1865. Although it suffered heavy bombing during World War II, the city later became a center of Italy's postwar economic boom. For example, Turin is the factory headquarters of the Fiat automobile company, which has produced millions of the small cars that crowd European streets.

Located on the fertile banks of the Arno River, Florence (population 453,000) is the birthplace of the Renaissance, a cultural movement that spanned the fourteenth through the sixteenth centuries. Artworks from this time period—such as Michelangelo's *David*—attract about one million tourists to the city each year. Contemporary Florence is home to many artists, who continue to produce fine handicrafts. Railroad, manufacturing, and communications industries also thrive in Florence.

Built in the center of a lagoon at the northern rim of the Adriatic Sea, Venice (population 306,000) was founded by refugees fleeing chaotic conditions on the mainland in the ninth century. The Venetians built their city by sinking thousands of heavy wooden pilings into the surrounding lagoon.

With streets closed to motor vehicles, commuters now use private boats, water-taxis, and long, black rowboats known as gondolas to travel from place to place. The Grand Canal, often jammed with small boats of every kind, winds through the center of the city. The many fine palaces, churches, and art galleries in Venice draw millions of visitors each year, making tourism by far the city's most important economic activity.

Photo © Elizabeth Buie

Shoppers examine fresh flowers at a bustling market in Turin, an industrial center in northern Italy.

Residents of Venice depend on gondolas and other boats to travel the narrow alleys—called *calli*—that run between the city's buildings. Many broad canals also cut through Venice, which lies on about 120 islands and a small part of the Italian mainland.

Dating to the sixth century B.C., this ear stud *(enlarged to show detail)* was made by an Etruscan jeweler. Expert gold workers, the Etruscans crafted intricate pieces for wealthy buyers throughout the Mediterranean.

Photo by The British Museum

2) History and Government

Italy was first settled thousands of years ago by hunters from northern and eastern Europe who crossed the Alps in search of game. The descendants of these people eventually spread down the length of the Italian Peninsula, stopping in fertile valleys to farm crops of grain and vegetables.

As early as 1200 B.C., the Etruscans arrived in northern Italy. They may have come by sea from some other region of the eastern Mediterranean or from Asia Minor (modern Turkey). Etruscan groups established 12 fortified city-states on the western plains of Italy—a territory that came to be called Etruria (modern Tuscany). Over time the Etruscans extended their holdings northward into the Po Valley and southward along the Tyrrhenian coast.

Skilled sculptors, potters, and metalworkers, the Etruscans traded goods with Greece, Egypt, and Phoenicia—a wealthy empire based in present-day Lebanon. Trading and mining created great wealth in Etruscan cities, which formed a federation ruled by elected kings and magistrates.

In the 700s B.C., Greeks seeking to escape overcrowded Greek cities left their homeland and settled in southern Italy and Sicily. This area, known to the Greeks as Magna Graecia (Greater Greece), was centered in Syracuse, a Sicilian city. The Greeks survived by trading consumer and agricultural products. Later colonists established cities along the coasts of Apulia, Calabria, and as far north as Neapolis, a port that later became the city of Naples.

Etruria to Rome

One of the wealthiest areas under Etruscan control was Rome—a populous farming region that covered seven hills along the Tiber River. Until the sixth century B.C., the Etruscan Tarquin dynasty (family of rulers) controlled the region. In 510 B.C., the Tarquin king was overthrown by the Senate—a body of Roman aristocrats who administered the city. The Senate founded a republic, in which two elected consuls served year-long terms as heads of state and as chief magistrates.

Etruscan rule remained intact outside of Rome for another 70 years, eventually weakening under the threat of foreign invasions. Unable to unite and stop the invasions, Etruria declined in power. By about 400 B.C., the armies of Rome had absorbed the area once held by the Etruscans and had added it to the republic's territory.

THE ROMAN REPUBLIC

The growing republic extended as far north as Tuscany and southward to Magna Graecia and Sicily. Backed by a large army, the Roman senate soon ruled the entire Italian Peninsula.

Roman society was divided between two classes—patricians (aristocrats) and plebians (common people). The patricians ran the government, made laws, and imposed taxes—mostly on the plebians. But the plebians gradually gained more power, helping to elect Rome's consuls. By 367 B.C., in fact, one consul was chosen from the plebian class.

In the third century B.C., Rome was threatened by the North African city of

Based in present-day Lebanon, Phoenician merchants *(above)* offered their wares to eager buyers in the Mediterranean region. The Etruscans and early Romans traded agricultural and mineral goods with the Phoenicians in exchange for luxury items from Greece.

Bringing several elephants to help break enemy lines, the Carthaginian general Hannibal led 60,000 troops in a surprise attack on Rome in 218 B.C., during the Punic Wars. Starting from Spain, Hannibal moved his army across France, over the Alps, and into Italy.

Carthage (in modern Tunisia). Armies from this Phoenician trading center crossed the Mediterranean to attack Sicily. This action sparked a series of wars against Rome that lasted for more than 100 years.

The clashes between Carthage and Rome—collectively known as the Punic Wars—featured invasions and counter-invasions. In 218 B.C., the Carthaginian leader Hannibal entered Italy from the north and destroyed Roman cities. The Roman armies fought back and defeated Hannibal. This victory allowed the republic to extend its authority to the Mediterranean islands of Sicily, Sardinia, and Corsica, as well as to the coast of northern Africa, including Carthage.

Never happy under Roman rule, the Carthaginians rebelled in 149 B.C., an event that prompted Rome to sack the city in the last Punic War. The end of the Punic Wars left Rome supreme in the Mediterranean. In addition to its previous holdings, Roman

military leaders added Greece and Egypt to the republic.

Rome's expanding colonial power brought great wealth to the patricians. But heavy taxation and land shortages caused revolts among plebians. A reform movement, led by the Gracchi brothers, organized rebellions in the streets of Rome. After reform attempts were squelched—and the Gracchis were assassinated—civil war erupted between Roman landowners and laborers.

THE ROMAN EMPIRE

The civil wars led to deep divisions within the Roman senate. Crassus and Pompey, senators who had helped to put down the revolts, formed a triumvirate (ruling association of three) with Julius Caesar, a successful Roman general. After the death of Crassus, Caesar defeated Pompey in battle and named himself the sole ruler of Rome. In 51 B.C., Caesar conquered Gaul (modern France), adding European lands west of the Rhine River to the Roman Republic.

Fearing Caesar's dictatorship, several of his former allies murdered him in 44 B.C. Thirteen years later, Caesar's nephew Octavian defeated rivals at the naval Battle of Actium, off the coast of Greece. The senate then proclaimed Octavian ruler of the Roman Empire.

Roman Rise and Fall

Under the name Augustus, Octavian ordered the building of new roads and public-works projects throughout the empire, which included most of Europe and the Middle East and parts of North Africa. His administration also established a uniform system of law for use throughout the vast domain. Roman culture and Latin (the language of the Romans) spread to the empire's far corners.

Augustus's successors reigned during the Pax Romana, a 200-year period when

Photo by Bettmann Archive

Considered a military genius in ancient Rome, Julius Caesar *(above)* helped expand the Roman Empire across much of Europe. Philosophers, musicians, and artists were attracted to the rich cultural life in Rome *(below)*, the capital of the empire.

Photo by Bettmann Archive

the realm enjoyed stability and peace. Laborers raised great walls and earthworks on the northern frontiers to protect Roman conquests. Fortifications were built along the Rhine and Danube rivers in central Europe for additional security.

Meanwhile, the new religion of Christianity was rapidly gaining popularity among Roman citizens, even though it was not legal. Victims of persecution under the early emperors, Christians had become a majority within the empire by the fourth century. A bishop, or local church leader, held authority in many Roman cities, including Rome. In A.D. 313, during the reign of Emperor Constantine, the Edict of Milan legalized Christianity.

Photo by Bettmann Archive

Romans flee their burning city in A.D. 410 during a raid by Visigoths from northern Europe. This attack signaled the beginning of the fall of the Western Roman Empire.

In 330 Constantine founded a second capital in Constantinople (modern Istanbul, Turkey) to provide an administrative hub for the empire's eastern regions. While the Italian Peninsula remained the center of the Western Empire, Constantinople became the seat of the Eastern Empire, later known as the Byzantine Empire.

Geographic divisions were not the only challenge, however. Waves of Goths and other Germanic peoples from northern Europe had begun to invade western and southern Europe. Their arrival—and their success in beating Rome's armies—caused the frontiers of the Western Roman Empire to shrink. In 410 an army of Visigoths overran Rome, looting the treasury and burning the capital's monuments. Roman rule soon ended in Gaul, Spain, and North Africa. The Gothic leader Odoacer overthrew the last Roman emperor in 476 and seized the leadership of the declining realm. By the end of the fifth century, the Western Empire had collapsed.

Byzantine and Lombard Rule

Despite the fall of Roman rule, Roman-style administration and culture survived in Italy. Many cities succeeded in absorbing the invading groups, who eventually accepted Christianity and adopted Roman laws and customs.

A new center of the Christian church was established in Constantinople. Christian leaders in Rome and Constantinople each developed different rituals and doctrines and became rivals for the loyalty of Christian worshipers throughout the empire.

At the same time, rulers of the Byzantine Empire sought to assert their control over the Italian peninsula and in the early sixth century successfully campaigned against the Goths. Ravenna, a city on the Adriatic coast, became the seat of Byzantine power in Italy, and the emperor Justinian officially made Italy a Byzantine province in 554.

The Byzantine emperor Justinian *(center, with bowl)* built churches, public buildings, harbors, and fortresses throughout his empire, which included the conquered territories of Italy, North Africa, and parts of Spain.

Within a decade, the Lombards, another Germanic group, had swept westward into the Po Valley from what is now Hungary. The Lombards founded a new capital in the north at Pavia and gradually settled throughout much of Italy. Lombard kings and dukes captured Ravenna, thus ending Byzantine rule in Italy. They then built a string of semi-independent states.

A strong rivalry developed between the Lombard kings and the pope, the leader of the Roman Catholic Church, which was based in Rome. Catholic popes had replaced the emperors as the rulers of Rome and its surrounding area and were using this region as a base for spreading the church's authority to the rest of Italy. But, without military force, the popes were unable to control the Lombard rulers.

In the 750s, as Lombard power grew, the popes turned to foreign rulers to defend Rome. Pope Stephen II asked for help from the Franks, whose kingdom included much of western Europe. Pepin, the Frankish king, defeated the Lombards and turned Ravenna over to the pope. Pepin's donation of lands became the basis for the Papal Sates, although these areas were not fully established until the sixteenth century. In 774, under Pepin's son Charlemagne, the Frankish armies overthrew the Lombard king and added Lombardy to Charlemagne's empire. In gratitude Pope Leo III crowned Charlemagne emperor of the Romans in 800. By this time, Charlemagne's kingdom extended from northeastern Spain and central Italy northward to Denmark.

To help strengthen the alliance between Charlemagne and the Roman Catholic Church, Pope Leo III crowned the Frankish king emperor of the Romans in 800. Throughout his reign, Charlemagne protected the church and helped increase its power.

After Charlemagne's death in 814, rivalries among his heirs caused turmoil. In 843 the Treaty of Verdun divided the Carolingian realm (Charlemagne's kingdom) among three descendants. For more than a century, the Carolingians fought one another for control of the kingdom.

Meanwhile, in the south, wealthy dukes and landowners continued to run their lands independently. The region was weakly defended, however, and in the ninth century Sicily, Sardinia, and the port of Bari on the southern Adriatic coast fell to Arab invaders from North Africa.

The Holy Roman Empire

Rivalry among princes and dukes for control of northern Italy brought foreign intervention in the tenth century. Fearing a loss of control over papal territories, Pope John XII crowned Otto I, the German king, as Holy Roman emperor and gave him charge of the Holy Roman Empire. In theory Otto was now the leader of Europe's Christian states, although most people in the empire also remained loyal to local princes. Through his alliance with the pope, Otto held authority over both church and state in most of Italy.

Later popes competed with the monarchs of Germany for control of Italian affairs. Although the German princes elected the German king, the pope crowned their choice as the Holy Roman emperor. In turn the emperor appointed the pope, the bishops, and other important church officials.

But many Catholics felt the church should name its own leaders without reference to Germany's royalty. A series of power struggles resulted between the monarchy and the papacy. A compromise between the Holy Roman emperor and church officials came about in 1122. The Concordat of Worms took the appointment of church officials out of the control of the emperors, who were still recognized as the legitimate civil rulers of Italy.

The City-States

The rivalry between the popes and the emperors left Italian cities on their own and allowed them to assert independence from both authorities. Through trading and banking, Milan, Florence, Venice, Genoa, and Pisa developed into wealthy city-states (or communes). Merchants and artisans within these city-states formed powerful political factions, which competed with farmers and aristocrats for control of communal governments. With their growing wealth and military power, the city-states were able to absorb surrounding estates and farmland and become entirely self-sufficient.

While these communal governments were rising in the north, most of southern Italy was still under the control of local Italian and Arab landowners. Farmers living on these lands paid as rent a large portion of their annual harvest, often owing annual military service to the landowner as well. In the eleventh century, Normans from northwestern Europe invaded Naples in southern Italy and drove out the Arabs. Later the Normans also conquered Sicily, establishing a kingdom in southern Italy in 1130.

The Normans held this realm only until the early thirteenth century, when a power struggle within the Holy Roman Empire caused its leader, Frederick II, to expand into Sicilian territory. A patron of the arts and sciences, Frederick set up his court at Palermo, Sicily, and dreamed of uniting the Italian Peninsula under his rule. His ambition quickly led to a clash with the pope, who had no intention of letting the Holy Roman Empire increase its authority over Italy.

After Frederick's death, the Catholic Church asked the French prince Charles of Anjou for help against Frederick's successors. Charles's armies took over Naples and Sicily. But in 1300, after a revolt by the citizens of Palermo, the French abandoned the island. Within a few years, the Aragonese dynasty, which ruled portions of present-day Spain, had also absorbed Sicily. Naples remained in Anjou hands.

Photo by Bettmann Archive

In 1231 the Catholic Church created the Inquisition, a court that investigated and punished heretics, or critics of Catholic teachings. At that time, heresy was considered an offense against the state as well as the church. The Inquisition operated mainly in Italy, Spain, France, and Germany.

The Renaissance

By the mid-fourteenth century, manufacturing and trade had made several city-states in Italy among the wealthiest communities in Europe. To glorify their achievements, the leaders of Florence, Rome, Venice, and other cities hired skilled artists to decorate homes, churches, and public buildings. Universities flourished in Padua and Bologna, where scholars translated the works of ancient Greek and Roman playwrights, philosophers, and historians. Italy's artists and writers turned to this classical past as inspiration for their works, resulting in a rebirth, or Renaissance, of art and learning that gradually spread to the rest of Europe.

At the same time, the governments of many communes were under the control of dictators, called *signori*. A few signori were appointed by the community, while some were invited to reestablish order after civil strife. Many signori founded family dynasties that remained in control for centuries.

Other city-states were guided by small groups of wealthy merchants. The Medici family, which ran an international banking business, was prominent in Florence. Venice, on the other hand, controlled a network of trading ports in the Adriatic and Mediterranean. The city's council, senate, and head of state (known as a *doge*) ran civic affairs. This system protected Venice's interests and brought the port many centuries of political stability.

Foreign Invasions

In the mid-fifteenth century, the drive to expand and control ever-larger territories brought the city-states into conflict with one another. Venice had absorbed Padua and Verona and then had founded an alliance with Florence, which had conquered Pisa and Lucca. To strengthen its position,

Photo by Erich Lessing/Art Resource, N.Y.

School of Athens (above)—a famous work by the Italian Renaissance painter Raphael—presents an imaginary gathering of ancient Greek philosophers and scientists. Renaissance artists had great respect for the classical culture of ancient Greece and Rome.

Photo by Bettmann Archive

Galileo Galilei, a learned astronomer and physicist, appeared before the Inquisition in 1616 to defend his belief in the theory that all planets—including the earth—revolve around the sun.

Milan allied with the Kingdom of Naples and Sicily, which had been united in 1442 under the Aragonese dynasty.

The Italian city-states signed the Treaty of Lodi in 1454 to settle their differences. The peace lasted until the 1490s, when Lodovico il Moro, the uncle of the duke of Milan, tried to seize his nephew's territory. To help his cause, Moro asked for assistance from the French king Charles VIII. An army of 30,000 French invaded Milan in 1494 and continued down the peninsula to Naples, where France exiled the Aragonese ruler.

Fearing French domination, several Italian states and the pope formed the League of Venice with the help of Spain and Germany. The league forced the French to retreat. Aragonese rule returned to Naples, but France held on to Milan.

For years French and Spanish armies fought for territory in southern Italy. In 1519 King Charles of Spain, who was a member of the Habsburg family, became Holy Roman emperor. As a result, from the start of Charles's reign, the Habsburg

Empire ruled Italy. By 1560 his heirs controlled most of the Italian Peninsula.

SPANISH RULE

Spanish rule was harsh. Italian cities struggled under the burden of growing taxes and heavy-handed administrators. Banking and manufacturing industries declined, and poor harvests brought outbreaks of famine and disease.

During the eighteenth century, the powerful states of Europe began to use Italy as a battlefield and its states as bargaining chips in an attempt to strike a balance of power among themselves. Gradually, Austria came to influence northern Italy, while Spain continued to hold the south. The Catholic Church remained in control of Rome and the Papal States.

NAPOLEONIC RULE

In the early 1790s, following a popular rebellion in France that had ended the French monarchy, Italy's republicans (people who favored representative government without a king) also rebelled. Italy's

Courtesy of National Gallery of Art, Washington, D.C., Samuel H. Kress Collection

The French general Napoleon Bonaparte conquered much of Europe in the late 1700s, creating a vast empire that included Italy. A strong administrator, Napoleon formed an efficient central government to rule his far-flung territories.

29

foreigners, powerful princes, and merchant families harshly put down the revolts. By the spring of 1796, however, republican armies under the French leader Napoleon Bonaparte had swept across northern Italy.

The new French government reorganized Italy. In place of many small city-states, Napoleon created the Kingdom of Italy, naming himself as king. He introduced a central administration and a uniform set of laws known as the Napoleonic Code. The kingdom seized church properties and large estates, built new roads, and established a centralized educational system.

But Europe's powerful monarchies could not allow Napoleon to succeed. Britain, Austria, Prussia (part of Germany), Russia, and Spain allied their armies and defeated Napoleon in 1815. The victors then met to divide up Italy. They agreed to return Lombardy and Venetia to Austria. Spain got back Sicily and Naples in the south. The dukes of Savoy gained Genoa and Piedmont (regions near present-day France), which, together with Sardinia, became the kingdom of Sardinia, later known as Sardinia-Piedmont.

Risorgimento and Unification

Many republican leaders were still determined to establish a unified, independent Italian state, however. They formed secret societies that conspired against the foreign-led administrations of Italy. This Risorgimento (reawakening) movement gained new members after the failure of popular revolts in southern Italy and in Savoy and Genoa.

A wave of republican rebellions swept across Europe in 1848 as workers, students, and revolutionaries stormed the streets of European capitals to demand representative governments. The unrest inspired workers in Venice and Milan to act, but Austrian armies forcefully put down the riots.

Although defeated the Italian nationalists did not give up. They turned to the independent monarchy of Sardinia-Piedmont, whose king, Victor Emmanuel II, supported Italian unification. An opponent of Austria, he saw unification as a way to give Italy its own voice, to oust Austria, and to gain some of Austria's holdings on the Italian Peninsula.

In the 1850s, Camillo Benso di Cavour, the prime minister of Sardinia-Piedmont, secretly negotiated with France, Austria's rival. In return for the regions of Savoy and Nice, the French gave military support to Sardinia-Piedmont. In 1859 forces from Sardinia-Piedmont and France defeated the Austrian army.

By the Peace of Villafranca signed by France and Austria, Austria surrendered Lombardy to France, which then ceded the region to Sardinia-Piedmont. But, al-

Giuseppe Mazzini, an Italian pro-independence activist exiled to France in 1830, formed an association called Young Italy to carry on the fight for a unified Italian nation.

though France had supported actions to weaken Austria, it did not approve of Italian unification. To Cavour's disappointment, important regions such as Tuscany and Emilia remained under the control of rulers allied with Austria. To express his dissatisfaction with this agreement, Cavour resigned.

Motivated to continue fighting for a republic, Italian rebels planned another revolt. Giuseppe Garibaldi organized a military band known as the Thousand. When rebellion broke out in Sicily, the Thousand sailed to the island and quickly overthrew its Spanish administration. Garibaldi then led the group on a march to Naples, forcing the Spanish to abandon the city.

Garibaldi's campaign sparked nationalist rebellions throughout Italy. Cavour returned to office in Sardinia-Piedmont and again negotiated with France. French officials agreed to support a new constitutional monarchy in Italy if the pope and Rome remained self-governing.

In October 1860, Victor Emmanuel II entered Naples, where Garibaldi proclaimed him king. By a popular vote, provinces in central and southern Italy joined the kingdom. The new Italian parliament announced the kingdom's founding on March 17, 1861. This new state included Sardinia-Piedmont, Sicily, and the entire Italian Peninsula, except for three areas. Rome was self-ruling but had the protection of the French military. Venetia stayed under Austrian control. And San Marino remained an independent republic.

Suddenly unified Italy began playing an important role in Europe's complex power struggles. When Austria faced off against the kingdom of Prussia in 1866, Italy allied with Prussia. The Prussian victory allowed the Italian kingdom to annex Venetia. Four years later, during the Franco-Prussian War (1870–1871), France withdrew its military from Rome. Italian troops quickly seized the city, which became the capital of Italy in 1871.

A champion of Italian independence, Giuseppe Garibaldi *(above, on horseback)* marched on Naples in 1860 to oust the city's Spanish administration. Garibaldi also led military campaigns in South America, earning him the nickname "Hero of Two Worlds."

Economic and Social Turmoil

Although Italy experienced changes in its governmental structure during the 1800s, the country remained largely agricultural and could not compete with the rapidly industrializing nations of western Europe. In the south, where the old system of landownership had survived until the early 1800s, poverty-stricken peasants still farmed meager holdings. Riots and crime became commonplace in southern Italy and Sicily, while millions of poor southern Italians emigrated to other European countries or to the United States.

Italy also suffered from a lack of political leadership. The kingdom's constitution gave only a small percentage of men from the upper classes the right to vote. This

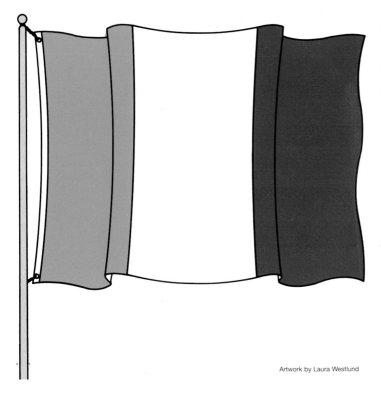

First used in 1796 by supporters of Napoleon, the Italian flag was designed to look like that of France, with green substituted for the French blue. Italy officially adopted the flag in 1870.

Artwork by Laura Westlund

group dominated the legislature without addressing the country's widespread social problems. In addition, Italy's politicians formed dozens of parties that constantly combined into different coalitions. With a wide variety of political beliefs, these groups could not agree on a common policy to improve the economy or the standard of living among Italy's workers and farmers.

New political factions, such as the Socialist party, established themselves with the support of farmers and urban laborers. Dissatisfied with the political system, these new organizations led strikes. Rioting among the urban poor shook Rome several times in the 1890s. Similar social unrest occurred in Sicily.

In 1901 Giovanni Giolitti, a liberal-minded reformist, became Italy's prime minister. Under Giolitti the Italian parliament legalized strikes, passed child labor laws, and limited the length of the work week. In 1912 the right to vote was extended to all adult males. (Women won this right in 1945.)

Giolitti also spearheaded economic changes, including large manufacturing industries in the north. At the same time, Italy sought to expand its power and territory by establishing colonies abroad. By 1912 Italy had taken over Eritrea (once part of Ethiopia) and Somaliland (present-day Somalia) in eastern Africa and had gained Libya in northern Africa.

World Wars I and II

The quest for colonies, land, and economic advantage sparked strong rivalries among the states of Europe during the late nineteenth and early twentieth centuries. By 1914 European powers had formed two major military alliances. The Triple Entente included France, Britain, and Russia. Italy joined the Triple Alliance with Germany and Austria. By this agreement, the three states pledged to defend one another in case of attack.

In 1914 the assassination of the heir to the Austrian throne sparked World War I

(1914–1918). In retaliation Austria attacked Serbia, a southeastern European nation that the Austrians believed was responsible for the murder. The war soon engulfed the two military alliances. German armies began fighting France and Russia. Italy chose to remain neutral, claiming that the Austrian attack was not an excuse for Italy's entry into the war. By the secret Treaty of London, signed in 1915, the Triple Entente promised Italy territorial concessions from Austria if Italy would enter the war on the entente's side.

The Italian government declared war on Austria in May 1915. Although Italian forces suffered defeat at the Battle of Caporetto in October 1917, the tide of war was turning against Austria and Germany. In November 1918, the Triple Alliance surrendered. The postwar Treaty of Versailles awarded Trieste and Trentino to Italy. But the treaty gave other regions that Italy had been promised to the new state of Yugoslavia on the Balkan Peninsula.

THE IMPACT OF MUSSOLINI

World War I had claimed hundreds of thousands of Italian lives. War debts burdened the Italian economy, while unemployment rose in the cities. In 1919 Benito

Photo by Corbis-Bettmann

From a trench, Italian troops look across "No Man's Land"—an unoccupied area between opposing forces—during World War I.

Mussolini, a war veteran and former newspaper editor, founded the political group Fascio di Combattenti (Band of Fighters). In his speeches and writings, Mussolini expressed anger toward the Italian government, which many Italians considered ineffective in foreign policy and in economic and social programs. Many workers agreed and joined Mussolini's fascist organization—a group that supported a rigid, conservative political system.

The fascist leader also found growing support among the middle classes and farmers. In 1922 Mussolini prepared a march on Rome. Fearing violence in the capital, King Victor Emmanuel III invited him to form a new government and to select a cabinet of ministers. Mussolini then proclaimed himself dictator of Italy under the title of Il Duce (the leader).

The fascists quickly reorganized the Italian state and took control of the economy. Public-works projects brought full employment to workers, while newspapers were censored and opponents of the regime were imprisoned.

By the 1930s, a fascist party under Adolf Hitler also had control of Germany. Mussolini sought an alliance with Germany as a means of expanding his empire. Italy invaded Ethiopia in 1935 and with Germany formed the Axis alliance the following year. The oppressive actions of Mussolini's government, however, made it increasingly unpopular among Italians. Strict press censorship, political repression, and persecution of Jews sparked increasing resistance to the fascist regime.

Hitler's own efforts to annex territory led to the outbreak of World War II in 1939. Italy at first remained neutral but in 1940 declared war on France and Britain—Germany's enemies and part of the anti-Axis Allies. The Italian army quickly suffered a series of military setbacks that rendered it nearly powerless during the course of the war.

In July 1943, the Allies invaded Sicily and quickly overran the island. Italians opposed to Mussolini's regime fought on the Allied side, pushing northward toward Rome. Parliament voted Mussolini out of

Photo by Moro Roma

The fascists—a group that favored strict government control of labor and industry—organized a march on Rome in 1922. The fascist movement, led by Benito Mussolini, at first had strong support among Italians.

In 1936 Mussolini *(left)* and the German dictator Adolf Hitler *(right)* allied their countries by signing the Rome-Berlin Axis, an agreement that outlined a common foreign policy for Germany and Italy.

Photo by Moro Roma

office, and Italy formally joined the Allies and declared war on Germany.

Determined to control the Italian Peninsula, German armies in Italy reinforced their lines and put up a stiff resistance. In heavy fighting, the Allied armies slowly pushed the German lines northward. In April 1945, Mussolini was captured and executed, and Hitler committed suicide. The next month, Germany surrendered.

Postwar Revival

In 1946 a national vote ended the Italian monarchy and founded the Italian Republic. But political turmoil continued. Debates and conflicts among Italy's many political parties frequently led to a change in government and to new elections.

By the late 1940s, the Italian political system came to be dominated by the Christian Democrat party, which included various coalitions. Socialists usually found themselves in a minority coalition. The Italian Communist party was strongly allied with the Communist-run Soviet Union and often won a greater percentage of votes than the Socialists did. Yet Communist party members were never invited into any governing coalition.

Fearing the growing power of the Italian Communists, the strongly anti-Communist United States extended massive amounts of financial aid to Italy to strengthen its majority government. This aid allowed Italy to rebuild its cities, industries, and transportation systems, all of which had been severely damaged in the

35

Workers in Turin examine cars as they roll off the assembly line in 1955.

war. The Italian government also set up a fund to develop southern Italy, which lagged behind the rest of the country in standard of living and economic growth.

Italy's links to the United States went beyond economic aid. In 1949 under Prime Minister Alcide De Gasperi, Italy joined the North Atlantic Treaty Organization (NATO), a military alliance of western European and North American nations. Italy also became a member of the European Economic Community (the present-day European Union), which lowered trade barriers among European member-nations.

Cheap labor and rising exports brought a boom in Italian manufacturing industries in the late 1950s and early 1960s. Busy factories in Lombardy and Piedmont pro-

duced steel for new building construction, appliances, and automobiles. Wages rose rapidly for workers, and a larger market helped farmers sell more of their produce.

But, in the mid-1960s, the Italian economy slowed. Heavy social spending by the government caused large budget shortfalls. And as wages rose, prices for goods went up and the standard of living began to stagnate. Communist and Socialist leaders who supported workers' rights were pushing for change and organized large-scale, antigovernment strikes in Italian factories. In national elections, these parties won high percentages of the popular vote.

In 1974 the country suffered a severe blow when the oil-producing nations of the Middle East prohibited oil exports, an action that caused fuel shortages, rising prices, and inflation throughout Europe. Italy also experienced a wave of terrorism at the hands of a number of radical political groups throughout the 1970s. The Red Brigades, for example, carried out bombings and kidnapped business leaders and politicians. The civil and economic chaos drew even more voters toward the Socialist party.

Recent Events

In 1983 Italy's first postwar Socialist government came to power under the leadership of Bettino Craxi, whose administration lasted until 1987. Throughout the 1980s, Italy's economy continued to grow despite inflation. By the early 1990s, however, many Italians were calling for fundamental reform of the political parties. The system of coalition governments seemed unable to cope with economic problems. In addition, a bribery scandal exposed corruption among many high-ranking politicians, business leaders, and judges. Despite hundreds of arrests and trials, many people believed that corruption remained commonplace among Italian leaders.

As the scandal widened, several new groups rose to challenge the traditional political system. These included the Lega

Supporters of Lega Nord (Northern League)—a group from northern Italy that seeks independence from the central government—carry flags at a political rally in the mid-1990s.

Photo © Massimo Sciacca

Nord (Northern League), composed of regional leaders in northern Italy who sought independence from the central government, and Forza Italia (Go, Italy!), a nationalist party led by business tycoon Silvio Berlusconi. In April 1994, a victory by Forza Italia allowed Berlusconi to form a new government.

Although the new prime minister announced measures to lessen the budget deficit, to reform the government, and to fight organized crime, he resigned in December when the governing coalition fell apart. An interim administration prepared for new elections, which were held in April 1996. College economics professor Romano Prodi won the prime ministership, backed by the Olive Tree Coalition—a group made up primarily of former Communists. His victory represents the first time since World War II that Italy has voted in a leftist, or liberal, leadership.

Government

The constitution of the Italian Republic was passed in 1947. The document established a 630-member chamber of deputies and a 315-member senate. Adults 18 years of age and older elect the deputies, while voters must be 25 to elect senators. Representatives of both houses serve five-year terms, but the number of seats held by each party is determined by the number of votes the party receives in national elections.

A two-thirds majority vote of the legislature chooses the president, who serves a term of seven years. The president has the power to promulgate (declare) laws and therefore is part of the legislative process. Additional presidential duties include serving as head of state and commander of the armed forces. The president can also call for special sessions of parliament and call for elections.

The Italian president appoints numerous positions within the government. For example, the president appoints the prime minister from the chamber of deputies. The prime minister, in turn, selects the members of the cabinet, who must be approved by parliament. The prime minister's other duties include directing government policy.

The cabinet and prime minister have no fixed terms of office, but parliament can pass a vote of no confidence in the govern-

Giulio Andreotti *(left)*, a seven-time prime minister, went on trial in 1995 on charges of collaborating with the Mafia while he was in power. Long a problem in Italy, the activities of the Mafia and other organized crime groups have ranged from international drug trafficking to corruption in awarding government construction contracts.

Italy's Parliament is made up of a 630-member Chamber of Deputies *(above)* and a 315-member Senate. The two houses have equal power in passing the country's laws.

ment and force it to resign. The president may also dissolve the government at any time. In either case, new elections are held.

Italy is divided into 20 regions, each of which includes provinces and communes. Elected councils and committees govern the provinces and elect a president. The regional councils have broad authority to pass laws affecting planning, taxation, and other matters, but these laws may be re-voked by the national government or the constitutional court.

The constitutional court includes 15 appointed judges, each of whom serves a term of nine years. This court rules on laws passed by the Italian parliament and by regional and local governments. Appeals courts hear civil and criminal cases from lower courts. Italy also has a system of tax courts and administrative courts.

Photo © Massimo Sciacca

During a sunny day at the park, a mother helps her daughter balance on a bicycle. Family activities are very important to Italians, who focus their social lives around extended family members, including grandparents, cousins, aunts, and uncles.

3) The People

Italy's population of 57.3 million has an uneven settlement pattern. The plains of Lombardy, Piedmont, and Lazio, for example, are densely populated, while the slopes of the Alps in the north, the Apennines, and southern Italy have notably fewer people.

Over the years, many rural villagers and farmers have moved into urban centers in search of employment. As a result, the rural areas of the country, especially in the southern regions of Calabria and Basilicata, have experienced a sharp decline in population. With about 97 percent of its people living in cities, Italy is one of the most heavily urbanized nations in the world.

Ethnic Groups

During its long history, Italy has been settled by many different peoples. Before the rise of Rome, Etruscans lived in northern and central Italy, and Greeks colonized the south. Germanic peoples arrived from the north in waves of migration after the fourth century A.D., and Normans built farms and cities in Sicily during the eleventh and twelfth centuries.

As a result, the ethnic heritage of Italian-speakers is mixed. It was not until the mid-1800s that an Italian nation existed, and many inhabitants still feel greatest loyalty to their region, town, or family.

About 2 percent of the Italian population is foreign born. Starting in the 1960s, various ethnic groups began immigrating to Italy. The newcomers were seeking work in the country's expanding economy. Foreign laborers from North Africa, Asia, and the Middle East have settled in Rome, Milan, Turin, and Genoa. Instability and war in the former states of Yugoslavia and

Albania have brought a large population of refugees, especially to southern Italy.

Religion

Roman Catholicism remains the dominant religion in Italy. About 95 percent of the population belongs to the Catholic Church, which plays an important role in daily life. Italian Catholics often turn to their priests and other church officials for advice and assistance. In addition, the church operates hundreds of schools and hospitals. Catholic charities also provide an important source of aid for workers, retirees, and the disabled.

Church doctrine once had a strong influence on the laws of Italy. A treaty signed in 1929 established Vatican City as the world center for Catholicism. Located entirely within the city of Rome, Vatican City is an independent city-state that is run by the pope and is not subject to Italian rule.

In addition to Catholics, Italy also has a small population of Jews, most of whom live in Rome and Milan. Albanian and North African immigrants follow the Islamic faith, and there is a small community of Italian Protestants.

Education and Health

After World War II, the Italian school system found itself unprepared for the task of educating the nation's growing population. A lack of facilities and teachers, as well as a disorganized educational network, contributed to the problems. Many elementary-aged children did not attend school at all, and others who wanted to enroll were too poor to afford basic school supplies.

During the 1960s, the government budgeted money to improve educational facilities and to hire many new teachers. School attendance rose, and illiteracy fell rapidly among school-aged children. By

Photo © Michael Kimak

St. Peter's Basilica—one of the largest Christian churches in the world—looms above a crowd gathered in Vatican City. An independent state ruled by the pope, Vatican City is the spiritual and governmental center of the Roman Catholic Church. About 95 percent of Italians are Roman Catholic.

An Italian teacher and physician, Maria Montessori designed an educational system in the early 1900s that focused on the development of children's intelligence and independence. Thousands of schools throughout the world use the Montessori method.

the mid-1990s, 97 percent of adult Italians could read and write.

Education is compulsory for children between the ages of 6 and 14. Students attend primary school from age 6 to age 11 and then go on to three years of lower secondary school. They then must pass a comprehensive examination to move to higher secondary schools, which are devoted to scientific, vocational, arts, and humanities studies.

After five years of higher secondary school, students take another test—the *maturita*—that allows admission to any Italian university. Italy has many universities, the oldest of which date to the eleventh century.

Before World War II, Italy suffered a shortage of hospitals and trained physicians. Public health improved dramatically with the economic boom of the 1950s and the 1960s. The health service now extends

Italian students listen to a classroom lecture.

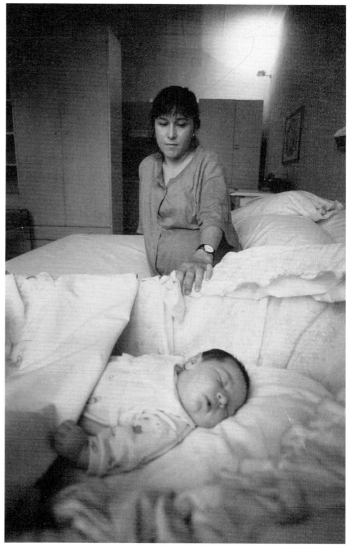

A mother watches over her sick baby in an Italian hospital. With one of the lowest population growth rates in the world, experts predict that Italy's population will drop by about three million people by 2025.

low-cost medical care, examinations, and medicines to all Italian citizens. In the mid-1990s, the rate of infant mortality—the number of babies who die within a year of their birth—was 8 per 1,000 live births, a figure below the European norm. Average life expectancy among Italians is 77 years, higher than the European average of 73 years.

The social-security system in Italy provides disability payments, unemployment benefits, and retirement pensions to Italian workers. The high cost of these bene-fits has led to widening government budget deficits, however, and many Italian leaders strongly favor cuts in social-security spending.

Language and Literature

Italian, like French and Spanish, is a Romance language with roots in ancient Latin. The language of the Roman Empire, Latin survived the empire's fall and became an international tongue of science, philosophy, and religion during the Middle

The bottom of a sign in the Alto Adige region of northern Italy welcomes visitors in three languages—Italian (right), German (center), and Ladin (left), a language similar to the Romansch tongue spoken by many Swiss.

Ages (A.D. 500–A.D. 1500). At the same time, the many separate regions and principalities of Italy developed their own local dialects, and the peninsula had no national spoken language until the late nineteenth century.

Modern Italian developed in the thirteenth and fourteenth centuries from the Florentine dialect. Centuries later the popularity of the language was boosted during the unification movement, when having a common language became a necessity.

Local dialects have still survived in many areas of Italy, including Sicily, Naples, and Venice. People who speak one Italian dialect do not necessarily understand those who speak another. In addition, foreign languages are used in several border areas. In 1992 the Italian government recognized Sardinian and Friulian (a northeastern Italian language) as official in their respective areas. German is common near Austria, and French is heard in Piedmont and in the Valle d'Aosta. Speakers of Slovenian and Croatian live near the city of Trieste. Many Albanian and Greek immigrants in southern Italy also use their native tongues.

Italy's literary tradition can be traced to the time of the Roman Empire, when writers such as Catullus, Horace, and Virgil wrote in Latin. Literature in the Italian language began with the works of thirteenth-century lyric poets, who used everyday speech instead of Latin to reach a wider audience. Dante Alighieri, a native of Florence who wrote *The Divine Comedy,* did much to establish the Florentine dialect as standard Italian among writers. Petrarch developed the poetic sonnet, and Giovanni Boccaccio collected 100 tales into his book known as the *Decameron.*

The Italian poet Dante Alighieri's most important work is *The Divine Comedy.* Written between 1308 and 1321, this epic poem focuses on the theme of life after death.

Italian artisans of the 1700s perfected the art of instrument making. Antonio Stradivari *(above)* is famous for his well-crafted stringed instruments, which he labeled Stradivarius—the Latin form of his name.

Writers of the 1500s expanded their range of subjects. In an age of complex rivalries and political scheming, Niccolo Machiavelli's *The Prince* described tactics for ambitious rulers. Baldassare Castiglione wrote *The Book of the Courtier* to guide his readers in proper manners at Italy's many aristocratic courts.

I Promessi Sposi, a nineteenth-century work by Alessandro Manzoni that was published during the Risorgimento movement, helped to spread the new standard Italian language to the country's readers. Gabriele D'Annunzio, a fervent Italian nationalist, wrote poems, plays, and novels that bridged the nineteenth and twentieth centuries.

After World War II, Alberto Moravia penned short stories and novels—including *The Conformist*—that described the problems of modern urban life. Giuseppe Tomasi di Lampedusa, the author of *The Leopard,* saw his tale of an old aristocratic family reach a worldwide audience in translation. Italo Calvino wrote *The Baron in the Trees* and other novels about improbable people and occurrences. One of Italy's most well-known contemporary writers is Umberto Eco. His complex novels, such as *The Name of the Rose,* delve into history, language, and philosophy.

Music

Italy has been an important center of European music since the early Christian era. Pope Gregory I fostered the development of the Gregorian chant in the sixth century. By the eleventh century, Guido d'Arezzo, an Italian monk, had worked out a system of musical notation that later developed into modern music writing. During the Renaissance period, new forms of secular music, such as the madrigal, arose in Italy.

In the 1600s, the Italian composer Claudio Monteverdi combined instrumental music, singing, and drama to create one of the world's first operas. The works of Alessandro Scarlatti and Antonio Vivaldi also challenged musicians during the Italian Baroque era. In the 1700s, Italian composers developed the sonata, a musical form that dominated European music for the next two centuries.

Jazz musicians perform at a café in Venice.

The Italian composer Giuseppe Verdi wrote 26 operas in the 1800s, including *Rigoletto, Il Trovatore,* and *La Traviata.*

Opera stood out in Italian music during the nineteenth and early twentieth centuries. Gioacchino Rossini's lively works include *The Barber of Seville* and *The Thieving Magpie.* Giuseppe Verdi, who wrote *Aïda, Otello,* and other masterpieces, promoted Italian nationalism in some of his music. Giacomo Puccini's *Madame Butterfly* remains one of the world's most popular operas. Gian Carlo Menotti, a contemporary composer, wrote *Amahl and the Night Visitors,* an opera often performed for children.

Although Italy has many venues for jazz, folk, and rock music, the contemporary music scene is still dominated by classical instrumental works and operas. Each year music festivals take place throughout the country, the most renowned of which is the annual festival of music and drama in the hill town of Spoleto in central Italy.

Art and Architecture

The art of the ancient Romans decorated private homes, public squares, religious buildings, amphitheaters, and palaces. Sculptors relied on familiar scenes from Greek and Roman mythology, while painters rendered portraits, landscapes, and still lifes. Roman architects designed massive temples, monumental arches, and public buildings, many of which remain intact. For example, the Pantheon, a meeting place built in the second century as a temple to the Roman gods, has survived in the center of Rome.

During the Renaissance period, Italian painters developed the science of perspective, which allowed artists to give more depth and realism to their works. Masaccio and Mantegna explored this new concept in their works, while Donatello brought lifelike emotions and poses to his sculptures. *La Gioconda* and other masterful paintings of Leonardo da Vinci were only a small part of his pursuits, which also included hundreds of inventions, armaments, and engineering works.

By the 1500s, Michelangelo was celebrated for his frescoes (paintings on plaster) in Rome. He was also noted for his powerful sculptures, including *David* and *Moses,* representations of biblical subjects. Raphael also painted frescoes, altarpieces, and portraits during this period.

At the same time in Venice, Titian, Tintoretto, and Giorgione were masters of oil painting. By 1600 the Baroque style of

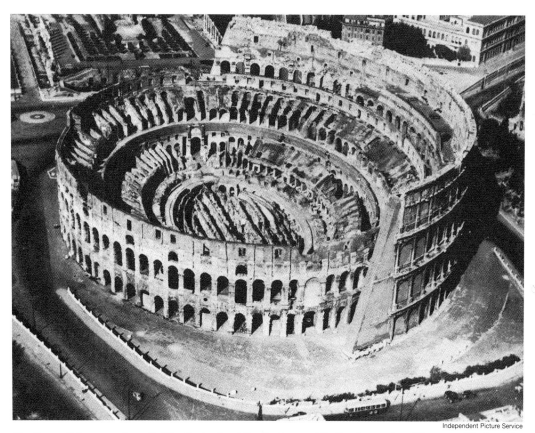

Independent Picture Service

The Roman Colosseum, also called the Flavian Amphitheater, is one of the finest examples of Roman architecture. The largest outdoor theater of ancient Rome, the Colosseum hosted public speeches and gladiator combats. In the Middle Ages (A.D. 500–A.D. 1500), residents removed more than half of the structure's original mass for building material.

The Renaissance artist Michelangelo laid on his back atop a scaffold for four years to paint the ceiling of the Sistine Chapel. The chapel is part of Vatican Palace. Each scene in this work depicts a story from the Bible.

Leonardo da Vinci's paintings *Mona Lisa* and *The Last Supper* are among the most famous works of the Renaissance period. Leonardo's scientific ideas—including a flying machine and a parachute—were ahead of their time.

painting—with its realism, detailed scenes, and rich colors—was developing in Rome. Caravaggio was known for his realistic portrayal of religious figures as well as for his masterful handling of light and shadows. The Baroque sculptor Bernini decorated Roman palaces and churches.

Italian art declined in importance during the later centuries, as new styles of painting were being developed in other parts of Europe. Giorgio de Chirico, a leading Italian surrealist of the nineteenth century, depicted dreamlike landscapes and symbols in his canvases. Amedeo Modigliani, a twentieth-century painter, is known for his modern portraits.

Built between 1385 and 1813, Milan's Gothic-style Cathedral is one of the largest churches in Europe. Each of the building's spires features a life-sized statue of a saint, a biblical character, or a historical figure. More than 3,000 statues decorate the interior and exterior of the cathedral.

Fans crowd stadiums throughout Italy to cheer their favorite *calcio* (soccer) teams.

Photo © Massimo Sciacca

Sports and Recreation

Italians enjoy a wide range of spectator and participant sports. The most popular professional sport is *calcio* (soccer). Led by Paolo Rossi, an international soccer star, Italian players are among the world's best. Soccer is also enjoyed by nonprofessionals, who play from childhood in a variety of leagues. A professional basketball league that hires players from around the world is gaining popularity in Italy.

Italian athletes have also excelled in Olympic competition. The Italian runner Gelindo Bordin won the marathon in the 1988 games, and downhill skier Alberto Tomba has carried home several gold medals in slalom competition at recent Winter Games.

Photo © Massimo Sciacca

Cyclists *(above)* find many challenging routes in Italy's countryside. Neighborhood pools *(right)* offer a place to cool off and relax in hot weather.

Photo © Massimo Sciacca

Two cooks fold pasta around meat and cheese fillings to make *tortellini,* which are boiled and served with a variety of sauces.

Italy's Alpine rivers provide fast-moving water for kayakers and canoeists, and ski resorts in the Alps and Apennines offer trails for downhill and cross-country skiers. Hikers enjoy a network of marked trails in the highlands. Sailors catch the wind off Tyrrhenian seacoasts and on the freshwater lakes of the north. Public tennis courts are common in Italian communities, and many new golf courses have been built near the largest cities.

Food

Meals are an important part of daily life in Italy. The dinner table traditionally has been the central gathering place for families, who celebrate events such as weddings, birthdays, and holidays with long meals lasting well into the night. But the modern workday has cut into leisure time. Even so Italians usually eat a light breakfast of coffee and bread or pastry, a large lunch taken in the early afternoon, and a small meal late in the evening.

Italian bakers are famous for their fresh bread.

Before a meal, cooks often serve a plate of appetizers, or *antipasti*. The plate may include *prosciutto* (ham), *formaggio* (cheese), and bread and olive oil. A soup or pasta dish may be served next. Many different sauces are made for pasta, which also comes in dozens of shapes and thicknesses. *Ragù* is a tomato-and-meat stew. Pasta *alla carbonara* is noodles prepared with egg, parmesan cheese, and ham. And pesto sauce is a mixture of olive oil, basil, garlic, and pine nuts. Common in northern Italy is a rice-based dish known as *risotto*. Italian wines are enjoyed at mealtime throughout the country.

Italians take pride in many regional specialties. Restaurants in Naples, the birthplace of pizza, prepare this popular dish with a variety of meats, vegetables, and sauces. Parma is known for ham and prepared meats, while Bologna, considered the country's culinary capital, is famous for *tortellini* (stuffed pasta) and Bolognese sauce. *Polenta* (a cornmeal dish) and risotto are common in Lombardy and Venetia. *Arancini* (deep-fried rice balls) and *marzipan* (a dessert delicacy made with almond paste) are Sicilian specialties. For dessert, many Italians enjoy cakes, pastries, or rich, flavorful *gelato* (ice cream).

Photo © Massimo Sciacca

An accordion player entertains patrons at a rural Italian restaurant.

Photo © Massimo Sciacca

Giant cranes load and unload cargo vessels at Genoa, Italy's largest and busiest port.

4) The Economy

Until World War II, Italy's economy was based primarily on agriculture. The postwar years brought rapid economic growth as the country began to industrialize. After joining European-wide trade associations, Italian industries expanded, and exports of manufactured goods soared. Turin and Milan became the principal manufacturing centers, while Genoa and Naples saw a rise in oceangoing freight traffic.

All regions of Italy did not share equally in the country's prosperity, however. Well-paying factory jobs were plentiful in the north, while many southern Italians struggled in agriculture or in small, family-owned workshops. In 1950 the economic imbalance prompted the government to establish the Cassa per il Mezzogiorno (Southern Development Fund) to encourage industrial growth in southern Italy. Although a few firms have relocated plants to this region, these plants recruit management and skilled labor from the north. Southern Italy lags well behind the rest of the country in economic development and standard of living.

By the 1990s, Italy had become one of Europe's most prosperous states, trailing only France and Germany in gross national product (GNP)—the value of goods and services produced by a country in a year. In 1996 Italy's estimated GNP had

54

reached $19,270 per capita and was increasing at a rate of 2 percent every year. Problems persisted nevertheless. Social spending caused rising budget deficits, and a system of generous annual wage hikes known as the *scala mobile* contributed to inflation. Although the scala mobile was abolished in 1992, the deficits left Italy with a huge public debt.

In addition, the Italian state controls much of the economy through large, inefficient holding companies that dominate important manufacturing sectors, such as energy and chemical production. Efforts to break up or to sell companies to private owners have largely failed. Yet the costs of running state-owned firms have left Italy with even greater debt.

Manufacturing

The growth of Italy's manufacturing sector in the 1950s and 1960s made the country a leading economic power in Europe. With financial aid from the United States, Italian companies built hundreds of new factories, which sold their products to a growing European market. Italian automobiles, appliances, machinery, and other manufactured goods were shipped across the continent. Joining the European Coal and Steel Community in 1952 and the European Economic Community in 1957 allowed Italy to greatly expand its exports.

Manufacturing now contributes about 20 percent of Italy's GNP and together with mining employs about 23 percent of the labor force. Northern Italy is still the home

A worker carefully layers olives, pasta, and other foods in decorative gift jars. Food processing makes up a large part of Italy's manufacturing sector.

of most large industries, which produce automobiles, computers, and chemicals. More than two-thirds of Italy's industrial workers have jobs in the north.

By the mid-1990s, machinery and automobiles had become the most important manufactured goods in the nation. The chemical industry, which is also strong in Italy, produces rubber, fertilizer, plastic goods, and industrial chemicals such as sulfur and ammonium. Textile and clothing factories in Milan and surrounding cities make Italy an international center of the fashion industry. The country also produces steel, appliances, and processed food.

Agriculture and Fishing

Once the mainstay of Italy's economy, agriculture now plays only a minor role. Most Italian farms are small, family-owned operations with less than 10 acres of land. Crops cover about 40 percent of the total land area. In hilly regions, farmers cut terraces into the hillsides to provide level growing land.

The principal crops in Italy are sugar beets, tomatoes, grains, grapes, and olives. In the Po Valley, farmers grow corn and irrigate their fields for rice production. Durhum wheat—the main ingredient of pasta—thrives in Campania, Tuscany, and

Photo © Massimo Sciacca

An assembler puts the finishing touches on a part for a motor scooter at an Italian manufacturing plant.

Photo © Massimo Sciacca

Farmers in northern Italy examine their cauliflower crop. Although some large, modernized farms operate in Italy, most agricultural land consists of smaller, family-owned plots that are planted and harvested using traditional methods.

Made from the juice of grapes—one of Italy's largest agricultural crops—wine is aged in wooden barrels *(left)*. **The wood contributes flavor to the wine.**

Emilia-Romagna (in north central Italy). Umbria and Tuscany produce olive oil, while orange and almond groves dot the hills of southern Italy and Sicily. Tomato vines and orchards of cherry and apricot trees are common sights in Campania. Grapes flourish in Chianti, Asti, and Orvieto, which are world-famous wine-producing areas. In fact, wine is one of the country's most important agricultural exports.

Although not a major force in the farm economy, livestock raising in Italy includes

Italian fishermen, who provide fresh fish to local markets, head out to sea to collect their daily catch.

An offshore refinery in the Adriatic Sea processes some of Italy's crude oil into fuel. Although Italy depends heavily on other countries for its energy supply, small oil reserves supplement imports.

beef and dairy cattle, pigs, goats, and chickens. Large sheep herds exist in the highlands of Sardinia, and goats are common in southern Italy and Sicily. Farmers pasture buffalo in Tuscany and Campania for meat as well as for their milk, which is used for making cheese.

The Italian fishing industry supplies the domestic market and draws on the fishing grounds of the Tyrrhenian and Mediterranean seas and the Atlantic Ocean. The largest catches are of swordfish, tuna, mullet, mussels, shrimp, squid, and octopi. Commercial fisheries also raise freshwater trout in inland lakes and rivers.

Energy

With few energy resources of its own, Italy depends on imports to supply more than 80 percent of its fuel needs. Most of these imports arrive from the Middle East and North Africa. A pipeline from Algeria, across the Mediterranean Sea, supplies more than three billion gallons of natural gas to Italy each year. As a result, the economy is greatly dependent on stable world market prices for oil and natural gas.

Italy's hydroelectric industry was one of the first in Europe. In the late 1800s, a new hydroelectric plant was set up to supply Rome with power. Fast-moving rivers in the north continue to generate energy. The country has also developed coal, oil-burning, and gas-fired electricity plants as well as nuclear power stations. In 1987, however, safety concerns and a public referendum forced the shutdown of one nuclear plant.

Italian companies continue to search for oil and natural gas within the country. Small offshore facilities have been built in

Ships dock at the port of Livorno, a major seaport and industrial center on the Ligurian Sea. Italy has one of the largest merchant shipping fleets in the world.

the Adriatic Sea and off the coasts of Calabria and Sicily. The country's largest natural gas fields are in the Po Valley.

Foreign Trade

Italy's position in the Mediterranean region has long made it a hub of international trade. For centuries Italy's cities exported textiles and other manufactured goods through busy ports such as Genoa and Naples on the Tyrrhenian coast and Venice and Bari on the Adriatic shoreline. After World War II, manufactured exports boosted the economy. By the 1990s, Italy was running a small trade surplus, as tourism and the sale of exports were bringing in more money than the country was spending on imported goods.

Italy imports machinery, transportation equipment, chemicals, steel, and electronic goods. Italy also buys much of its meat from abroad. Fuels make up more than one-fifth of the value of the country's imports. The United States, Britain, France, Germany, and the Netherlands are the largest sources of imported goods.

Italy exports food, automobiles, office equipment, electronic goods, clothing, shoes, leather items, textiles, and steel. Principal foreign customers for Italian products are the United States, Japan, and the countries of the European Union—including France, Germany, Britain, and Spain.

Transportation and Tourism

Italy has well-developed road, rail, air, and water networks. After World War II, a massive program of road building linked the country's villages and cities. Southern regions—once served only by gravel and dirt roads—benefited the most from this program. A 4,000-mile system of express highways—or *autostrada*—now runs between major urban centers. Italian road planners are also considering a bridge that will link the Italian mainland with Sicily.

Italy's railroad system dates to the late nineteenth century, when the newly unified Italian government made a large investment in modern rail lines. Travelers can journey from northern to southern Italy within a day on *rapido* and *espresso* routes. Slower *diretto* and *locale* trains stop at smaller towns and cross the Apennines, connecting Rome with the Adriatic coast. Bus lines serve remote villages.

Passenger ferries link the mainland with Sicily, Sardinia, and the Lipari Islands in the southern Tyrrhenian. International ferries run to Greece from Bari and Brindisi on the southeastern coast and from Sicily to the island of Malta to the south. Commercial cargo is transferred at Naples, Genoa, Palermo, and Bari.

Many of Italy's major cities have international airports. Milan's Malpensa Airport is the country's busiest. Leonardo da Vinci Airport, outside Rome, is a hub for flights linking Europe to the Middle East and Africa. The national airline Alitalia operates both domestic and international routes.

Tourism has become one of the largest sectors of the Italian economy and is an essential source of income for many Italian businesses and workers. Millions of tourists

arrive each year from all over the world to visit the country's cities, museums, historic sites, and recreational areas. Venice alone welcomes several million tourists annually. In fact, in the summer months,

Run mostly by the government, Italy's railroad lines *(above)* carry passengers and freight between the country's major cities. Tunnels through the Alps link Italy's modern highway system *(left)* to those of neighboring countries.

A popular tourist attraction, the Leaning Tower of Pisa is the bell tower of the Cathedral of Pisa, which Italian builders put up as three separate structures. Built on unstable land, the tower began to sink and lean as it was being constructed between 1173 and 1370.

Photo © Gino Russo

the city's year-round inhabitants often make up a minority of the population.

Rome attracts foreigners to its extensive ancient ruins and magnificent churches, while Florence offers many treasures of Renaissance painting, sculpture, and architecture. Naples boasts an impressive archaeological museum and the ancient towns of Herculaneum and Pompeii. Music lovers make a pilgrimage to La Scala, Milan's famous opera house. Buildings from the Middle Ages and the Renaissance

Photo © Galyn C. Hammond

Mount Vesuvius looms above the ruins of Pompeii, a seaport in southwestern Italy that was covered by a thick layer of ash from the volcano in A.D. 79. Thousands of visitors tour the excavated city each year.

Siena's Gothic architecture draws many visitors, who often start their tour of the city at the Piazza del Campo *(above).* **Es-tablished during the Middle Ages on the scenic hills of western Italy, Siena once rivaled its northern neighbor Florence as a center of trade and industry.**

are preserved at Assisi, Perugia, Siena, and San Gimignano in the central highlands.

The Future

A complex and sometimes chaotic nation, Italy overcame many of its historic divisions and built itself into a European economic power. But Italian society still faces serious problems. Unemployment, pollution, and crime plague many cities, and political scandals have damaged public trust in the country's leaders. Hundreds of business-people, judges, and local officials are fac-ing trial on a variety of corruption charges.

If Italian companies can maintain growth in production and in exports, the country's economy will continue to provide jobs and a rising income for Italian work-ers. The heads of Italy's political parties must overcome a more difficult challenge. They are facing widespread cynicism on the part of voters and challenges from new, more radical parties. A worsening economy or social conflict may trigger a larger cri-sis in the Italian government or even a re-turn to regional self-rule. As a result, the country's future stability and prosperity depend on the ability of politicians and business leaders to regain public trust.

Index